THE BEHAVIOR TECHNICIAN

STUDY GUIDE

Covering the Task List 2.0

Fluency Questions

Glossary

ABA Study Guide
BCBA® Mock Exams and Study Prep

website: *https://abastudyguide.com*

e-mail: *behaviorwebinars@gmail.com*

Published by Beluga Publications, Nacogdoches, TX

THE BEHAVIOR TECHNICIAN

STUDY GUIDE

Jaime Flowers, Ph.D., BCBA, NCSP

Table of Contents

Introduction

My name is Dr. Jaime Flowers. I am a professor at Stephen F. Austin State University. I also provide a RBT course online. While providing the 40-hour online course to people, I found many students struggling to find quality study material for the RBT exam. I created this study guide to help students studying for the RBT exam. It follows the RBT task list exactly, and it contains everything you need to pass the RBT exam.

This manual will go over each task list item. There are fluency fill-in questions after every section. There is also a glossary. My hope is that this study guide provides you the support you need to pass the RBT.

Measurement

Preparing for data collection

Data collection is an important part of an RBTs job. Supervisors and families rely on RBTs to collect valid data to help make programming decisions. Without valid data no one will be able to determine if a student is making progress. Data collection allows us to determine when and if a student is making progress.

Task Analysis of Data Collection

1.) Determine the type of behavior you are collecting data on, such as duration, rate, interval.

2.) Determine the best data collection method. Your supervisor will help. This is often outlined in the functional behavior assessment or the behavior intervention plan.

3.) Gather the materials you need to collect data: paper, pen, clipboard, timer, data collection sheet, and sometimes, an electronic method.

4.) Fill out any identifying information needed. This could include name, birthdate, setting, date of observation, time of observation, diagnosis, and the behaviors or skills being observed. If there is no standard fill-in form, write it on the top of your data sheet.

5.) Try to eliminate distractions.

6.) Begin collecting data.

Fun fact: The word data is plural—you would not say "the data is". Rather you say "the data are".

Continuous Measurement Procedures

Continuous measurement means measuring each and every instance of behavior within the observation period, missing nothing. This type of measurement is very time-consuming and more difficult than discontinuous measurement procedures.

Types of Continuous Measurement

Frequency: This is a simple count of the instances of behavior, represented by a tally. *How many times did John hit another student?* You would tally every time John hit another student and present the count as a number. *John hit 5 times.*

Rate: Rate is a frequency count with a time element. If you were tallying how many times John hits another student you would also report the time. *John hits at the rate of 5 times per hour.* Rate is an important measurement when looking at behaviors which are frequent and short. For example: hitting, raising hand, flapping hands, disrupting another student, yelling.

Duration: This is how long a behavior occurs. To take duration data you start a stopwatch when the behavior begins and end the stopwatch when the behavior stops. Duration is often reported as an average over time. Duration recording is appropriate for long lasting behaviors. For example, tantrums, social play, how long it takes a student to get dressed.

Inter Rate Response: This is the time between responses. To take IRT data you start the stopwatch when the behavior ends and stop the stopwatch when the behavior begins again. IRT is typically reported as an average. IRT is appropriate when the time between behaviors is important. For example: time lapse between doing math problems, and time lapse between prosocial behaviors.

Latency: Latency is the time from prompt to the start of the behavior. To take latency data start the stopwatch when the prompt is given and stop the stopwatch when the behavior starts. You might want to take latency data when there is a delay between the prompt and when the behavior occurs. For example, the time from a prompt to get dressed to a student getting dressed, the time from the instruction to begin a math problem and the response.

Discontinuous Measurement Procedures

Discontinuous Measurement Procedures are samples of the target behavior, but they do not measure every instance of behavior within the observation period. Discontinuous measurement procedures are less valid than continuous measurement procedures. Discontinuous measurement procedures are used when it is too time-consuming to take continuous measurement data. With all interval data collection procedures the observation is broken up into intervals (i.e. 10 seconds, 20 seconds, 1 minute). Your supervisor will select the interval you should use.

Partial Interval: Recording the presence or absence of a behavior during a brief interval of time. Intervals are marked as "+" if the target behavior occurred at any time during the interval. Intervals are marked as "-" if the target behavior did not occur during the entire interval. Partial Interval data collection overestimates the occurrence of behavior. Examples of behaviors that are appropriate for partial interval recording are vocal stereotypy, hand flapping, biting nails.

Whole Interval: Recording the presence or absence of a behavior during the whole interval. Intervals are marked as "+" if the target behavior occurred during the entire interval. Intervals are marked as "-" if the target behavior stopped at any time during the interval. Whole Interval data collection underestimates the occurrence of behavior. Examples of behaviors that are appropriate for whole interval recording are cooperative play, social engagement, on task behavior.

Momentary Time Sampling: Recording the presence or absence of a behavior at the very end of an interval. Intervals are marked as "+" if the target behavior occurred at the end of the interval. Intervals are marked as "-" when the target behavior does not occur at the end of the interval. This procedure is possible to do for many students at the same time. This is the easiest type of discontinuous measurement procedure to use. However, it provides the least amount of information. Examples of behaviors that are appropriate for whole interval recording are social engagement of many students, and task engagement for a group of students.

Permanent Product Procedures

Permanent product recording is not recording behaviors but recording the products behavior produces. For example, you could record how many questions a student answered on a worksheet by simply looking at the worksheet and counting the problems completed. The advantage is you can record information from permanent product anytime. The disadvantage is you are not actually recording behavior. For example, a parent could complete a math worksheet for a student and you would not know if you were only recording permanent product.

Examples of permanent product recordings
1.) How many items were placed on a shelf.
2.) How many math problems were completed.
3.) How many bracelets were constructed.
4.) How many dished cleaned.
5.) How many scratches a student has.

Enter Data and Update Graphs

Recording data is an important part of an RBTs job. You should receive directions from your supervisor on how to accurately collect and graph data. Graphing can be done with a pencil and paper or a computer program.

How to Summarize Different Types of Data
1.) Frequency is summarized as rate over sessions
2.) Duration is summarized as total duration over session
3.) IRT is summarized as an average.   * Inter Rate Response *
4.) Latency is summarized as average latency to response
5.) Interval data is summarized as percent intervals with occurrence.

Rules for Graphing

1.) Label the horizontal axis with sessions or days
2.) Label the vertical axis with the type measurement you are using
3.) Graph one data point for every session
4.) Draw a solid line connecting data points in the same phase
5.) Draw a vertical phase line to separate phases of treatment
6.) Do not connect data points between different phases
7.) Use different symbols to depict different behavior on the same graph
8.) Use a legend or written names with arrows to label the different behaviors if more than one behavior is depicted on the same graph.

Fluency Questions for Measurement

1.) Sally is recording a student's behavior. She starts the stopwatch when the student begins screaming and stops the stopwatch when the student stops screaming. What type of measurement procedure is she using? _Duration_

2.) Paul wants a quick and easy way to record 5 different students' task engagement. What type of measurement procedure should he use?
Momentary Time Sampling

3.) Tony reported his data collection as a percentage of intervals with occurrence. What type of data collection is he using? _Discontinuous Measurement Procedure or Interval Procedure_

4.) A student of Mary's takes a very long time to start getting dressed after instruction. What type of data collection would be appropriate?
Latency

5.) Tom does not have a lot of time to collect data on a student's social engagement during play. What type of measurement should he use?
Whole Interval Recording

6.) Harry wants to record how many times his student hits. He should use a _Frequency_ count and report the data as _Rate_.

7.) An interval recording procedure that overestimates behavior is
Partial Interval Recording

8.) _Continuous_ measurement is the most valid and preferred type of data collection.

9.) Recording the number of pieces of clothing a student folded is called _Permanent Product Recording_

10.) Paul starts a stopwatch when a behavior ends and stops the stopwatch when the next behavior begins. This is called _IRT → Inter Rate Response_

Assessment

Behavior in Observable Measurable Terms

Operational Definition: Detailed definition of the behavior in observable terms. Must be thorough enough that any student could read it and understand what the behavior looks like and begin collecting data on the behavior.

> **Objective.** Operational definitions only include directly observable aspects of behavior (e.g., hitting), not unobservable internal states (e.g., frustration).

> **Clear**. Operational definitions should be unambiguous. Anyone, without any prior knowledge of the behavior, should be able to understand the definition. A good test is that a student who has never seen the behavior can collect data from just the definition.

> **Complete**. The definition includes all of the information necessary for you to discriminate between the behavior and other behaviors that are similar but do not count. Including specific examples and non-examples is often helpful.

> **Individualized.** The particular forms of a behavior that one individual display will likely be different from those of another. For example, Jimmy's aggression might include hitting and kicking, whereas Sally's might include pinching and scratching

Examples

> 1.) Lying on the floor, crying, yelling, throwing objects, and/or pounding fists on desk. The episode is counted if it lasts 10 seconds or more and is counted as a new incident if separated by 5 minutes or more.
> 2.) Student is looking at the teacher/board/seatwork, contributing to the assigned task, and quiet when expected to work independently.

Preference Assessments

Preference Assessment

A set of procedures used to determine if one or more stimuli may function to increase the rate of a specific behavior or behaviors when delivered following the occurrence of that behavior. You are trying to determine which reinforcers are most effective. Preference assessments are done during the assessment process and throughout the course of therapy.

Free Operant Preference Assessment

The therapist does not interact with the student. The therapist observes which items the student interacts with and records the time spent with the item. This is a simple observation procedure with no manipulation. The student can freely choose which items to play with or use. The items are ranked by the amount of time the student spent with them.

Single Item Preference Assessment

The therapist simply presents one item after another. The therapist records whether the student consumed/interacted with the item, made no response to the item, or avoided the item. For food items a small piece is presented, and for non-food items the student is allowed to interact with the item for 30 seconds. The amount of times a student interacted with an item is counted. The items are ranked by the amount of times a student interacted with them.

Paired Choice Preference Assessment (Forced Choice Preference Assessment)

The therapist presents 2 items to the student and records which item the student chooses. Allow the student to interact with the item for 30 seconds. All items should be randomly presented in pairs. This forces a choice from the student and is useful when the student interacts with most items during a single item preference assessment. The items chosen the most are ranked as stronger reinforcers.

MSW

Multiple Stimulus Preference Assessment with Replacement   MSW

The therapist presents multiple items at a time and records which item the student chooses to interact with. Allow the student to interact with the item for 30 seconds. Once the item is chosen the therapist places it back into the mix of multiple items. The downside of this method is the student can continually pick the same item over and over again not providing a ranking order of reinforcers. No more than 7 items should be presented. This is a good choice of preference assessment for students who can scan an array.

MSWO

Multiple Stimulus Preference Assessment without Replacement   MSWO

The therapist presents multiple items at a time and records which item the student chooses to interact with. Allow the student to interact with the item for 30 seconds. Once an item is chosen the therapist does not place it back into the array.

Individual Procedures

RBTs will help their supervisor assess where their student's ability is in social skills, language skills, academics, self-help skills, daily living skills, job skills, coping skills, etc. . Much of ABA therapy is working on building these skills so that a student can have an independent and successful life.

Baseline: Baselining is finding out where a student's skills or behaviors are before beginning therapy. Before beginning to teach a new skill, a baseline probe should be conducted in order to identify whether the student already has the skill. Present a prompt and record the student's response. Typically, three to five baseline data points will be sufficient, but your supervisor will guide you as to how much data to take.

Skill Assessments: Skills assessments determine where a student's skills are. They typically assess areas such as social skills, coping skills, self-help skills, language skills, learning skills, daily living skills, communications skills. Often these assessments come as packaged product. The most commonly used skill assessments in ABA are: Verbal Behavior Milestones Assessment and Placement Program (VB-MAPP), Assessment of

Basic Language and Learning Skills—Revised (ABLLS-R), and Vineland Adaptive Behavior Scales 3rd edition (Vineland-3).

Curriculum-Based Assessment: Curriculum-based assessment (CBA) and curriculum-based measurement (CBM) are the repeated, direct assessment of targeted skills in basic areas, such as math, reading, writing, and spelling. An example of a CBM is measuring how many words a student could read in a minute. A therapist would give the student a grade level passage and have the student read the passage out loud. The therapist would record how many words the student read correctly per minute.

Social Skills: Social skills are skills used to communicate and interact with people. Social skills include receptive and expressive language, and non-verbal communication.

Daily Living Skills: These are skills that people use every day to function. They include hygiene and grooming, dressing and undressing, meal preparation and eating, moving around the community, toileting, housekeeping, laundry, and safety skills.

Assist with Functional Assessment Procedures

RBTs also assist with functional behavior assessment (FBA) procedures. These are procedures designed to determine the function of maladaptive behaviors so that therapists can work on reducing the maladaptive behaviors and increasing prosocial behaviors.

Functional Behavior Assessment (FBA): A functional behavior assessment is a set of procedures used to determine why someone is engaging in a problem behavior. FBAs are typically done prior to beginning ABA therapy. RBTs may help their supervisors' with FBA procedures.

Indirect FBA Procedures: Part of an FBA may include record reviews, interviews, and rating scales. There is very little contact with the student during indirect procedures. These procedures can often be done with the family and caregivers of the student.

Direct FBA Procedures: Part of an FBA will include direct observations and skill assessments. These procedures involve observing the student and recording what is seen. There are many types of observation procedures. An RBT could be asked to take rate, duration, IRT, latency, or an interval recording on a behavior to determine the baseline of the behavior. This means that the RBT will determine how often the behavior is occurring prior to beginning therapy. An RBT can also be asked to take ABC (antecedent, behavior, consequence) data.

Functional Analysis Assessment: This is when a Behavior Analyst manipulates the environment to determine the function of the behavior. RBTs will not be asked to conduct these types of assessments but an RBT may be asked to help. The supervisor on the case will provide you with directions.

Antecedent Behavior Consequence Data Collection (ABC): This is a type of data collection in which you record what happened before the behavior occurred (antecedent), record what the behavior looked like (behavior) and record what happened immediately after the behavior (consequence).

Fluency Questions for Assessment

1.) An _Operational Definition_ is a detailed description of the behavior in observable terms.

2.) ABC data is collecting the _Antecedent_, behavior, and _Consequence_.

3.) Nancy wants to do a preference assessment in the quickest time possible, she should use _Multiple Stimulus Preference Assessment_

4.) If Tom is interviewing the parent of a student, he is using _Indirect Assessment_.

5.) Paul wants to manipulate the environment to determine the function of the behavior, he should use _Functional Analysis Assessment_

6.) Nick is getting a rank order of reinforcers by showing his student 2 reinforcers at once and recording which reinforcer they prefer, he is using _Paired Choice Preference Assessment / Forced Choice_

7.) _Skills Assessment / FBA_ assessment measures a student's self-help and vocational skills while _Functional Beh. Asses_ determines the function of the behavior.

8.) Larry is doing an ABC observation of his student, what type of FBA is he doing? _Direct FBA_

9.) Maria wants to observe her student interacting with reinforcers, she should use _Free Operant Preference Assessment_

10.) Tim is showing his student an array of reinforcers, when the student interacts with a reinforcer Tim removes it from the array. Tim is using — MSWO _Multiple Stimulus Preference Assessment without Replacement_

Skills Acquisition

Identify the Components of a Skills Acquisition Plan

A behavior intervention plan (BIP) or behavior reduction plan (BRP) is a set of procedures to reduce maladaptive behaviors. A skills acquisition plan is a set of procedures to increase the skills of the student. These skills can be in multiple areas but are typically in social skills, self-help skills, community skills, daily living skills, and vocational skills. A skills acquisition plan will outline the goals for a student and how a therapist will teach the goals.

Components of Skills Plan

        1.) Overall Goals for students

        2.) Instrumental Goals for students (steps to reach the overall goals)

        3.) What type of technique should be used to teach the skill?

        4.) What type of prompting should be used?

        5.) What is mastery of the goal (how many times does the student need to perform the skill without prompting to determine mastery)?

        6.) What type of reinforcement strategies will be used?

        7.) A plan for generalization and maintenance.

Preparing for a Session

When an RBT is starting a therapy session there are a few steps to take. Typically, an RBT takes about 15 minutes at the beginning of a session to prepare.

1.) Review notes from previous session
2.) Minimize distractions
3.) Gather reinforcers
4.) Gather materials
5.) Read the skill plan as a reminder of the goals and techniques required

Contingencies of Reinforcement

Reinforcer: Any consequence that increases a behavior. For example, if you give a cookie to the student who is screaming, *I WANT A COOKIE*, the student is more likely to scream in the future to receive a cookie.

Punisher: Any consequence that decreases a behavior. For example, if you reprimand a student for jumping on the couch, the student is less likely to jump on the couch in the future you have punished the student.

Unconditioned Reinforcement: The effectiveness of the reinforcer is not dependent on the learning history. In other words, things we are born wanting such as food, water warmth. Also known as primary reinforcers. Examples: food, water, warmth, pleasure, air.

Conditioned Reinforcers: The effectiveness of the reinforcer is dependent on the learning history. Things that differ from one student to another, such as music, specific types of food, electronics. Also known as secondary reinforcers. Examples: electronics, money, toys.

Positive Reinforcement: Positive reinforcement is adding something to the environment to increase the future probability of the behavior occurring. For example, giving a student a cookie for cleaning up toys, giving a student a hug for saying thank you, or giving a student screen time for doing math work.

Negative Reinforcement: Negative reinforcement is removing something from the environment to increase the future probability of the behavior occurring. For example, you will put your seat belt on to cease the annoying seat belt warning noise in your car, student cries when he sees math homework so the homework is removed in the future the student is more likely to cry if she sees math homework.

Positive Punishment: Introducing something that will increase the future probability that the behavior will decrease. Examples: You touch a hot pot and your hand gets burned, in the future you are less likely to touch a hot pot.

Negative Punishment: Taking something away that will increase the future probability that the behavior will decrease. Example: a student yells out in class and the teacher takes away a token, the student is less likely to yell in the future.

Continuous Reinforcement: This is a schedule in which the therapist reinforces every correct response of the target behavior.

Intermittent Reinforcement: This is all other schedules when reinforcement does not occur after every response. This schedule is less prone to extinction, or the behavior stopping. For example: giving reinforcement every 3 responses or giving reinforcement about every 5 responses.

Fixed Ratio (FR): Providing reinforcement on a fixed response ratio. In other words, if you were providing reinforcement on FR2, every 2 times the student correctly responds they would be providing reinforcement. If you were providing reinforcement on FR5, every 5 times the student correctly responses they would be providing reinforcement.

Fixed Interval (FI): Providing reinforcement on fixed time schedule. You provide reinforcement on the first correct after an interval of time. If you were using FI3, you would provide reinforcement on the first correct response after 3 minutes had passed. If you were using FI5, you would provide reinforcement on the first correct response after 5 minutes had passed.

Variable Ratio (VR): Providing reinforcement on a variable (average) response ratio. In other words, if you were providing reinforcement on VR2, on the average of 2 correct responses the student correctly responses they would be providing reinforcement. A VR3 schedule would look like this: reinforce after 1 response, 3 responses, 5 responses. The average of 1, 3, and 5 is 3, so it is a VR3.

Variable Interval (VI): Providing reinforcement on a variable (average) time ratio. You provide reinforcement on the first correct after an average interval of time. If you were using VI3, you would provide reinforcement on the first correct response after an average 3 minutes had passed. The schedules might look like this: reinforce first correct response after 1 min, 3 min, 5 min. The average of 1, 3, and 5 is 3, so it is a VI3.

Implement Discrete Trial Training Procedures

Discrete Trial Training (DTT) is among the most well-researched and well-known treatments and educational procedures for teaching skills to students with ASD. DTT is a teaching method in which learning trials are presented in quick succession, with a clear beginning and clear end to each trial. There are three parts to a discrete trial:

1. The instruction delivered by the therapist,
2. The student's response,
3. The consequence delivered by the therapist.

Immediately after the first trial a new trial begins. The advantage of DTT is that it produces rapid learning. The disadvantage is that sometimes a student does not generalize the skills to other environments.

Implement Naturalistic Training Procedures

ABA therapy can also be embedded within play or every day routines. A variety of types of naturalistic teaching procedures have been developed and shown to be effective with students with ASD. Naturalistic teaching procedures are known by several names including: natural environment training, pivotal response training, milieu teaching, incidental teaching, multiple exemplar training, etc..

All Naturalistic Training Procedures share these common features:

1. Student directed learning
2. Reinforcers are related to the teaching and environment
3. Motivation imbedded in the teaching or play
4. Interspersed mastered skills.

An example of naturalistic training would be to teach the student colors and animals noises through play. If you have a farm toy you could use the cow toy to teach the word cow. You might move the cow into the barn and say, *What just went into the barn?*. The student would respond with *cow* and you would praise the child and continue by saying, "The cow is hungry now, move the cow to the hay". In this example the student is demonstrating both receptive and expressive language skills.

Implement Task Analyzed Chaining Procedures

Task Analysis

Breaking a complex skill or series of behaviors into smaller, teachable units, the product of a task analysis is a series of sequentially ordered steps.

Example: Task Analysis for Brushing Teeth

1.) Get out toothbrush and toothpaste
2.) Wet toothbrush and apply toothpaste
3.) Brush the outside surfaces of the upper teeth
4.) Brush the chewing surfaces of the upper teeth
5.) Brush the inside surfaces of the upper teeth
6.) Brush the outside surfaces of the lower teeth
7.) Brush the chewing surfaces of the lower teeth

8.) Brush the inside surfaces of the lower teeth

9.) Brush the tongue using small strokes

10.) Rinse mouth

11.) Rinse toothbrush

12.) Put away toothbrush and toothpaste.

To create a task analysis you can use one of the following methods:

- Observe a competent individual perform the task
- Consult with experts or students skilled in performing the task
- Perform the task yourself.

Behavior Chain: A sequence of behaviors that must be performed correctly. The steps are taught sequentially to a student. It allows the student to learn complex skills that require many small steps.

Forward Chaining: Training begins with the first behavior in the sequence. The student learns to perform the first step independently, the therapist completes all other steps. Training only occurs on the steps previously mastered and current step (no training on steps after that).

Backwards Chaining: Training begins the last behavior in the sequence. The therapist performs all but last step until the student masters that last step. Then the therapist performs all but last two steps until student masters last two steps, and so on.

Total Task Chaining: Training is provided for every behavior in the sequence during every training session. Therapist assistance (prompting) is provided on every step.

Implement Discrimination Training

Discrimination Training: This procedure involves reinforcing one behavior and extinguishing another behavior (not reinforcing). For example: a student would receive a cookie if they said *red* in the presence of a red car; however, they would not receive a cookie if they said *red* in the presence of a green car. A student would receive a high five if they said *Mom* when their mom walked in the room and would not receive a high five if they said *Mom* when their dad walked into the room.

Discriminative Stimuli (SD): A stimulus in the presence of which a particular response will be reinforced. Example, if a student would receive a cookie if they said *red* in the presence of a red car, the red car is the SD. A student would receive a high five if they said *Mom* when their mom walked in the room, mom is the SD.

S-Delta: A stimulus in the presence of which a particular response will not be reinforced. For example, a student would receive a cookie if they said *red* in the presence of a red car; however, they would not receive a cookie if they said *red* in the presence of a green car, the green car would be an S-Delta.

Stimulus Control Transfer Procedures

Stimulus Control is acquired through stimulus discrimination.

Stimulus Generalization: Occurs when stimuli that share similar physical characteristics with the controlling stimulus evoke the same behavior as the controlling stimulus. For example, a student calling all dogs *Bella* because the student's dog is named Bella or a baby calling both Mom and Dad *dada*.

Stimulus Discrimination: Occurs when new stimuli – similar or not similar – to the controlling stimulus do not evoke the same response as the controlling stimulus. For example, a student would receive a cookie if they said *red* in the presence of a red car; however, they would not receive a cookie if they said *red* in the presence of a green car.

Implement Prompt and Prompt Fading Procedures

Prompting is a cue or hint meant to induce a student to perform a desired behavior. There are many different types of prompts. There are also different ways to fade prompts.

Physical prompt: A prompt in which you provide some amount of physical assistance in order to help the student do the expected behavior. Physical prompts can be further classified by the amount of physical assistance given. **Full physical prompts** are giving the student full physical guidance. For example, when teaching a student to wash their hands, you might deliver the instruction, immediately followed by placing your hand over the student's hand and moving them the running water. A **partial physical prompt** is a physical prompt in which less than the full amount of physical assistance is provided. In the example just described, a partial physical prompt might be to gently push the student's hand to the running water and then letting go of the student.

Model Prompt: A prompt in which you demonstrate the desired response. For example, when teaching a student to wave when greeted, you may show her how to do this skill by doing so yourself.

Verbal Prompt: Supplementary words, instructions, or questions to assist a student's in demonstrating a correct response are called verbal prompts. For example, when teaching a student to wash the dishes you might remind them of a step (e.g., *Remember to dry the dish*). Verbal prompts can also be full or partial.

Gestural Prompt: A prompt where you indicate the correct response by gesturing in some way. For example, when asking a student to pick out the red car you might gesture to the red car.

Proximity Prompt: A prompt where the stimulus that corresponds to the correct response is placed closer to the student than other stimuli. For example, if you were teaching the color blue, you would provide the direction and then place the blue object closer to the student.

Visual Prompt: Often used to help students with transitions and schedules. For example, you might create a visual schedule that depicts the sequence of events to take place during a therapy session.

Least-to-Most Prompt Fading: Includes procedures where fewer prompts are provided at the beginning of a teaching and gradually more intrusive prompts are faded in when the student needs help.

Most to Least Prompt Fading: This prompt works in the reverse direction. With MTL prompt fading, you begin the teaching interaction by providing a prompt that you are sure will help the student make the correct response; then you fade the prompts out.

Time Delay Prompt Fading: You can also insert a time delay that occurs after instruction but before the prompt. A student might reach for his iPad. You would withhold the iPad until the student made a vocalization. You would wait 3 second between withholding the iPad and giving a prompt for the vocalization.

Generalization and Maintenance

Generalization: Spreading the effects of training to other settings, which is important so that students are able to benefit in multiple settings. There is two types of Generalization:

1.) Stimulus Generalization: The behavior that occurs in the presence of one stimulus also occurs in the presence of another stimulus. For example, teaching a student to say *dog* when they see a Newfoundland, then the student says *dog* when they see a Maltese A student learns to identify their sibling's emotions and then begins to identify friend's emotions.

2.) Response Generalization: When one behavior occurs in the presence of a stimulus and then another behavior occurs in the presence of the stimulus. For example, you teach a student to build a castle with blocks and he builds a house with the same set of blocks.

Maintenance: Probing the student to ensure that they still are able to do mastered skills. If the student mastered labeling the color red, you would check that the student could still say *red* in later sessions.

Implementing Shaping Procedures

Shaping is defined as differentially reinforcing successive approximations toward a terminal behavior. The general rule is that you are reinforcing any behavior that is a closer to the target behavior than the behavior you reinforced last. For example, if you wanted a student to say *ball* you would first reinforce a b sound, once the student had mastered a b sound you would reinforce a *ba* sound and finally reinforce the full word *ball*.

Token Economies

Token economies are reinforcement systems that employ a monetary system (token reinforcers) and backup reinforcer. Token economies can be used to control a wide range of behaviors. Token economies typically use diverse consequences. For example, a student earns a star sticker every time they raise their hand. After earning 5 star stickers the student is able to choose a toy from a treasure chest in the classroom.

Fluency Questions for Skills Acquisition

1.) Matt is providing 20 minutes on a tablet every time his student engages in prosocial behavior. His student loves being on his tablet. Matt is providing _Positive Reinforcement_.

2.) If a therapist uses a delay to determine if a student can do a skill independently, and if the student needs help the therapist prompts, it is called _Time Delay Prompting_.

3.) Harry is removing a token every time his student hits him. Harry is providing _Negative Punishment_.

4.) Martha is providing a treat every time her dog sits. Martha is providing _Continuous Reinforcement_

5.) Martha stops providing a treat every time the dog sits, and provides a treat after the dog sits three times. Martha is providing _FR3 Intermittent Reinforcement_

6.) Carrie is using a visual schedule for a student. She is using _Visual Prompting_.

7.) Reprimanding a student is typically _Punishment_.

8.) Positioning the correct card closer to a student is called _Positional Prompting_.

9.) If a therapist starts by providing the most prompting in the beginning and slowly fades the prompts as the student becomes sufficient at the skill, it is called _Most to Least Prompting_

10.) Physically moving the student to a toothbrush is called _Physical Prompting_.

11.) Breaking a task into smaller pieces is called _Task Analysis_.

12.) Reinforcing one behavior in the presence of a stimuli and not reinforcing the behavior in the absence of that stimuli is called _Discrimination training_

13.) If Tom does not reinforce his student saying *ball* in the presence of a truck, the truck serves as the _S Delta_.

14.) If Callie is doing all the steps of a chain with a student, but training the student to do the last step independently, she is using ___Backward Chaining___

15.) If Tom reinforces his student saying *ball* in the presence of a ball, the ball serves as the ___SD - Discriminative Stimuli___

16.) If Ginger is giving her student quick learning trials presented in quick succession, she is using ___Discrete trial Training___

17.) If Ginger starts teaching her student through play, motivation, choice, and interspersing mastered skills, she is using ___Naturalistic Training Procedures___

18.) If a student must master the first step of a chain before moving on to the next step it is calling ___Forwards Chaining___.

19.) If Vera says the first part of the correct answer for her student, she is using ___Verbal Prompting___.

20.) Paul models the correct skills to his student, he is using ___Model Prompting___.

Behavior Reduction

Identify the Essential Components of a Behavior Intervention Plan (BIP) or Behavior Reduction Plan (BRP)

Teaching skills is the most important part of an ABA program. However, reducing behavior is also important. Problem behavior often occurs when teachers and parents have been attempting to skill build with a student. When a therapist starts skill building with the student problem behaviors will sometimes occur. Behavior reduction program tells you what to do when the behaviors occur.

Components of Behavior Reduction Plan

1.) Operational definition of the behavior
2.) Function of behavior
3.) Antecedent strategies to address the behavior
4.) Replacement behaviors
5.) Consequence strategies to address the behavior
6.) People responsible for the plan
7.) Emergency measures.

Functions of Behavior

The four functions of behavior tell us why someone in engaging in behavior. Depending on the function of the behavior you will use different techniques to reduce the behavior. This will all be written into the behavior plan.

Access to Something in the Environment: Sometimes this is broken into 2 functions: attention and tangibles. In simple terms, a student is engaging in behavior to gain something positive in the environment. This can be anything: attention, cookies, screen time, toys, activities, a place, etc. Anything you can see or do in the environment could be the reason a student is engaging in behavior. An example is when a child cries in the checkout line at a supermarket to get a candy bar.

Escaping Something in the Environment: A student engages in behavior to escape something aversive in the environment. Again, this can be anything—escaping math homework, food, a location, a student, etc. An example of this is when the teacher presents a hard math problem and the student runs out of the room.

Access to Something in the Body: This is sensory behavior. It is engaging in behavior to gain something positive in the body. Everyone engages in sensory behavior, such as biting nails, twirling hair, or tapping fingers.

Escaping Something in the Body: This is also known as pain attenuation. This refers to ~~Pain Attenuation~~ engaging in behavior to escape something aversive in the body. Taking a Tylenol™ when you have a headache is an example of pain attenuation. Scratching an itch is another example—you relieve discomfort in your body by scratching. When a student is engaging in pain attenuation is it important that the student sees a physician so that all medical issues are taken care of.

Implement interventions based on modification of antecedents such as motivating operations and discriminative stimuli.

Antecedent interventions happen prior to the problem behavior occurring. These interventions will modify the environment so that a student is less likely to engage in problem behaviors.

Establishing Operations: This refers to instances when something is made more valuable by deprivation—if you are hungry you are more likely to engage in food-seeking behavior. The hunger or being deprived of food is the establishing operation. You can increase the value of a reinforcer by depriving a student of the reinforcer prior to the start of therapy. For example, if you use an iPad as a reinforcer, have the caregivers of the student not allow the student to have the iPad 24 hours prior to therapy starting.

Abolishing Operation: This is when something is made less valuable by satiation. If you are full you are less likely to engage in food-seeking behavior. The feeling of fullness is the abolishing operation. You can decrease the value of a reinforcer, which was maintaining maladaptive behavior by satiating a student of the reinforcer. For example, if the student cries for attention from mom, you can have mom continually provide attention on a fixed time schedule (i.e. every hour mom provides 5 minutes of undivided attention). This will decrease the value of attention to the student (i.e. the student is getting plenty of attention) and decrease the behavior of crying.

Non-Contingent Reinforcement: This is providing reinforcement to a student regardless of behavior. This will act as an abolishing operation on the reinforcer. For example, providing a student 5 minutes of attention every hour, this will make is less likely for the student to engage in maladaptive behaviors for attention. Providing a student 5 minutes of screen time every hour, will make is less likely for the student to engage in maladaptive behaviors for screen time. Providing a student a 5 minute break every hour, will make it less likely for the student to engage in maladaptive behaviors to escape something aversive.

Demand Fading: This is a technique where you increase the demand over time. This is best used with behaviors which have the function of escape. For example, first presenting a small amount vegetable and increasing it over time or first presenting one math problem and increasing the amount of problems over time.

Task Modification: This technique is changing how the student does work. This is also used for behavior with the function of escape. Making it more preferred by the student. Examples: using a favorite character for counting, allowing the learner to use a favorite pencil, and identifying real objects rather than pictures of objects.

High Probability Sequence/Behavior Momentum: Providing 3-4 demands (directions) with high compliance (you are sure the student can and will do them), and presenting the demand (direction) with low compliance (student often does not follow the direction) at the end of the sequence. This must do this quickly; keeping the demands simple. Due to compliance in the first part of the sequence, the student "rolls" into compliance in the last part of the sequence. Examples: bite of pasta, bite of pasta, bite of pasta, bite of vegetables, several easy math problems followed by a hard math problem, and putting on several pieces of clothing which are easy, and then putting on the harder piece of clothing

Choice: Giving the student a choice during therapy, choice increases compliance and provides the student a sense of control. Examples: *Which color should we use? Which game should we play ? Which animal do you want?*

Implement Differential Reinforcement Procedures   DRO/DRI/DRA/DRL

Differential reinforcement procedures are when a therapist reinforces replacement behaviors. A replacement behavior is a prosocial or good behavior that can take the place of a problem behavior. There are a couple types of replacement behaviors.

Differential Reinforcement of Other Behavior (DRO): Reinforcing another behavior   DRO other than the problem behavior. The "other" behavior (can be anything) is reinforced if the problem did not occur for a specific amount of time.

Differential Reinforcement of Incompatible Behavior (DRI): Reinforcing a behavior that   DRI cannot physically be engaged in at the same time as the problem behavior. For example, reinforcing hugging instead of hitting (a student cannot hug and hit at the same time), reinforcing hands in pocket instead of pinching (a student cannot have his hands in his pocket and pinch at the same time), or reinforcing singing instead of yelling (a student cannot yell and sing at the same time).

Differential Reinforcement of Alternative Behavior (DRA): This is reinforcing a behavior   DRA that meets the same function of the problem behavior. For example, if the student is tantruming for attention you could reinforce asking to play a game. Both tantruming and asking to play a game will gain attention. If a student is running away to escape homework, you could reinforce asking for a break. Both running away and asking for a break will allow the student to escape the homework.

DRL

<u>Differential Reinforcing Lower Rates of Behavior (DRL):</u> This is typically reserved for behaviors that are socially acceptable but may occur too often. Using this procedure, reinforcement is delivered if a behavior occurs below a lower rate. For example, James uses socially appropriate behavior to greet peers but does so up to ten times in one class period (i.e. James keeps saying "hi" to his friends over and over again). His teacher decides to use DRL to lower the rate of his behavior, but she does not want to eliminate it completely, saying "hi" is a good behavior. She decides to deliver reinforcement (e.g., computer time) to James if he greets peers five or fewer times during the class period. If he greets peers more than five times, he does not receive reinforcement. The teacher would slowly reduce the amount of times James can say "hi" to gain reinforcement until he says "hi" at a typically level.

Implement Extinction Procedures

<u>Extinction</u> is removing whatever was reinforcing the problem behavior. Extinction procedures are always used with differential reinforcement. If you are going to reduce a problem behavior you must increase an adaptive or good behavior. Extinction should not be used until antecedent procedures and differential reinforcement has been tried.

<u>Attention Extinction:</u> Also known as planned ignoring. Ignore the behavior and provide no attention for the behavior. You need to keep students and staff safe. Do not laugh, look at or engage with learner until the behavior is over. Immediately provide attention once the behavior is over and praise them for calming down, using words, etc.

<u>Tangible Extinction:</u> Do not provide access to the item during the behavior. This type of extinction is very easy to do, just keep item out of sight. Stay strong, behaviors can escalate when student knows they will not get item. For example, when a student cries for a candy bar in the supermarket do not give item to student.

<u>Escape Extinction:</u> Do not allow the student to escape. Physical prompt the student into compliance. Your supervisor will give you directions on how to physical prompt. Typically, you'll either prompt through a small portion of the demand and then reinforce heavily, or you continue until the learner does the demand without the behavior.

Example: *Clean your room*, student tantrums, therapist physical prompts student to pick up the toys on the floor until they stop the tantrum.

Implement Crisis/Emergency Procedures According To Protocol

When a student engages in behaviors which pose a threat to others emergency procedures will be used. It is important that you follow the emergency procedures in place. Examples: restraints, protective equipment, or moving the student to another environment. Emergency planning is the job of the supervisor. Your supervisor will train you on the plan. Always communicate changes in behaviors and whether the plan is working.

If you can, ask for help before the situation becomes a behavior emergency. When a student is aggressive towards you, you may have negative emotions towards them. This is natural. You must always act professionally despite these feelings. There is never an excuse for aggression towards a student. No matter what your student's behavior, they always deserve dignity and respect from the professionals who work with them.

Emergency behavior management training, or restraint training: There are many commercial trainings available: Pro-ACT, CPI, Safe Schools. These trainings will teach you how to restraint students in a safe manner. These are different than the individual student emergency protocol. Your supervisor or the agency you work for should arrange so that you are trained in these procedures.

Fluency Questions for Behavior Reduction

1.) Mike provides reinforcement to his student when his student raises his hand 3 times a class, but not when his student raises his hand more than three times a class. This is called _DRL - Differential Ranforcement of a Lower Rate_

2.) The procedure to use when a student is hurting themselves or others is called _Behavior Emergency Plan_

3.) If a student is engaging in behavior to avoid an aversive activity, is it called _Escape Behavior_

4.) When Molly hits her head on a wall because she has a headache, she is engaging in _Pain Attenuation_

5.) Mickey provides attention to a student for 5 minutes every hour, this is called _Non Contingent Reinforcement_

6.) Reinforcing shaking hands instead of hitting is called _DRI_ of incompatible behavior.

7.) Pete increases his student's compliance by adding a favorite character to a worksheet. This is called _Task Modification_

8.) Rafael's student does not like to pick up his toys. Rafael provides the following directions to his student, *give me a high five, jump high, clap hands,* and finally *pick up toys.* This is called _Behavior Momentum_   - 3-4 Demands

9.) When you twirl your hair, you are engaging in _Sensory Behavior_

10.) A plan that states what to do when a student engages in problem behavior is called _Behavior Reduction Plan_
Behavior Intervention Plan

Documenting and Reporting

Effectively communicate with a supervisor on an ongoing manner.

You need to communicate effectively with your team (supervisor, and other RBTs). When there are 2 RBTs working one program they need to keep each other informed on how each session went. You will need to discuss the goals you worked on, behaviors you saw, what reinforcers you used, any extra materials you needed, and ecological or environmental variables affecting the therapy.

Often your supervisor will hold team meetings for a specific student. This may or may not include caregivers. It is important that you communicate clearly about the case in these meetings. It is also important that you help the process by ensuring time is used wisely. This is not the time to bring up other work-related issues. This time is to discuss the progress of the learner and any changes that need to be done to program.

Seeking clinical direction

When you have questions about students or therapy you need to seek support from your supervisor. It is very important this is done in a timely manner. A good rule of thumb is to ask a question for a non-emergency situation within 24 hours, to allow your supervisor sufficient time to answer the question before your next session with the student.   It is always good to check in with your supervisor even about smaller issues during therapy, as long as you are contacting them about therapy or work-related issues. A good supervisor wants as much information about progress and status of the therapy.

Reporting ecological variables

You need to report things that may affect the therapy session. Typically, these are reported in the notes section. We call these ecological variables. Examples of ecological variables:

1.) Changes in student's medication
2.) Student is ill
3.) Student didn't get enough sleep
4.) Student missed a meal
5.) Student spent the weekend with another caregiver.

A caregiver might tell you something that is subjective such as *He was at his dad's and his dad just gives him cookies for dinner.* Though this could be true you did not observe it. You still report this but you would write *Mom reports that Johnny spent the night at his dad's and his dad gave him cookies for dinner.* Whenever you are told something you write it by saying _____ *reported that .... "*

Generate objective session notes

Generating session notes is an important part of a RBTs work. You are often the person who sees the student the most besides the caregiver on the team. You must report what you see in a professional objective manner. There should be a notes section for you to complete at the end of each session with the student.

It is critical that you use professional language when documenting notes. The parents will have access to the notes section. Write exactly what you see or hear, not what you think or feel. Always be mindful of the reader. Don't say *Johnny was bad today* say *Johnny engaged in 3 counts of hitting, and 4 tantrums.* Don't say Johnny didn't like the rewards, say *Johnny's behavior continued despite increasing reinforcement.* Don't say *Johnny was anger*, say *Johnny said I'm angry and hit 5 times today.*

Each setting (student population, school or private, city, county, state) has its own unique set of laws and regulatory requirements. Each funding source has different requirements. Your supervisor should review this with you. These requirements can affect many different parts of your therapy such as note takings, length of therapy, what areas you can work on with the students, etc...

An incident report is a formal document in which you report something unusual during therapy. Most common is injury to staff member by student. For example, is a learner bites through the skin of an RBT, drawing blood; you would make an incident report. Another example would be if a learner falls down and bruises his knees.

Comply with applicable legal, regulatory, and workplace data collection, storage, transportation, and documentation requirements.

The applicable laws about confidentiality are Family Educational Rights and Privacy Act (FERPA) and the Health Insurance Portability and Accountability Act (HIPAA) Privacy Rule.

Any data with the learner's identifying information should be kept confidential. You should never allow anyone but the team members and the caregivers to view these type of documents. When using electronic data everything needs to be uploaded to confidential data base. You supervisor will give you more directions.

Typically, a student might have a binder with data sheets, and program information in it. This item might be moved around to the home, back to the office, etc. You must move this item quickly and only leave it in a location with a lock. This type of materials should only be in secured locations. A secure location is in a locked room, in a locked cabinet

Fluency Questions for Documenting and Reporting

1.) If a student fell and hurt both their knees badly you would complete a
Incident Report.

2.) _Team Meetings_ are important because everyone involved in therapy meets to discuss progress.

3.) If you have a clinical question, you should ask your supervisor within
24 Hours.

4.) _Professional language_ is important because the caregivers of the student could read your session notes.

5.) _Ecological Variables_ are things outside the therapy that may be affecting the progress.

Professional Conduct and Scope of Practice

Describe the BACB's RBT supervision requirements and the role of RBTs in the service-delivery system.

RBT implement the skills plan and behavior plans designed by BCBA. You should not be designing or creating plans. If you are unclear of what to do with a student you should ask for assistance. Your opinions and experience are relevant because you often spend the most time with the learner. But the BCBA has specialized training to create plans; if you have ideas share them with the BCBA. Have your BCBA tell you the appropriate time to share these ideas. Do not add these ideas without permission from the BCBA. This can create inconsistency within the program.

Respond appropriately to feedback and maintain or improve performance accordingly.

All people are capable of learning. This applies to staff as well.

Behavioral Skills Training: Is the most researched based technique. BCBAs are trained to use this method to train staff.

1) Instruction: provide a description of the skill, its importance or rationale, and when and when not to use the skill. Repeat this step as necessary. Show your participant how to perform the skill.

2) Modeling: In-vivo modeling is recommended. Other options are using video modeling.

3) Roleplay: Practice, practice, practice! Allow the participant opportunities to practice the skill. Recent research suggests that participants should be able to practice *in situ*. The trainer should record data on correct and incorrect responding during this step.

4) Feedback: The trainer should provide positive praise for correct responding and some form of corrective feedback for incorrect responses.

Decades of research show BST can improve work performance. You should receive immediate, specific positive feedback when you are doing things correctly. Beyond *Good job*; more like *You delivered that prompt with perfect timing*. Feedback should tell you exactly what you did correctly. When you are implementing techniques incorrectly you should receive immediate, specific, corrective feedback. This should include a verbal explanation and modeling.

No one likes to receive feedback. Try to look at feedback as an opportunity to improve your skills. No one is perfect. Try not to take it personally. Keep in mind that it is not about you personally, it is about delivering the best possible services to the student.

Your supervisor should also help you work towards long-term and short-term goals. Examples might be delivering immediate and contingent reinforcement, collecting accurate data, and implementing extinction. There should be regular checks on your progress with these goals. You supervisor should provide immediate feedback on your progress with these goals. This part of supervision.

Communicate with stakeholders (e.g., family, caregivers, and other professionals) as authorized.

You will often need to communicate with stakeholders. Your job is to implement, not make decisions. When asked a question not within your role as an RBT politely let them know the BCBA on the case will contact them with an answer.

Inappropriate Questions to Answer:

- Rationale behind a part of the BIP
- How a procedure might be modified
- Future plans for the student
- Ethical justification for procedures.

If you are unsure, tell the parent that your supervisor will call them, and inform the supervisor. You are representing the school or company you work with, so it is important that you do not say anything that the director of the company or the BCBAs working at the company would not say. You do not have authority to make decisions for students.

Maintain professional boundaries (e.g., avoid dual relationships, conflicts of interest, social media contacts).

You may be in close contact with family members of students, especially in home-based programs. You may find the family members begin to treat you as a family member. You should treat them courteously but remember to maintain a professional relationship. Do not allow your relationship with the family member to become something other than a professional relationship.

The Ethics Code states a <u>multiple relationship</u> is *one in which the behavior analyst is in both a behavior-analytic and a non-behavior-analytic role simultaneously with a client, supervisee, or someone closely associated with or related to the client*; this is harmful because the caregivers and student are depending on you as a therapist.

If you enter into a multiple relationship and the relationship ends badly the student probably will not want to receive services from you anymore. Social media often causes multiple relationships—"friending" parents and family members is not appropriate. It could cause HIPPA breaks and unprofessional communication. It also could affect your relationship depending on what you post personally.

Maintain student dignity.

Student dignity is of the upmost importance. You should always treat a student in the same manner you would want to be treated, or treat the student in the same way you would want your child, brother or sister treated. Use respectful language when addressing the student, and speaking about the student. For example, *Johnny loves lining up objects,* not *Johnny has autism, so he lines up objects*. Do not call someone a *spitter* or a *biter*.

Many people with disabilities are unable to advocate for themselves; so they may be suffering in silence. Your job is to increase communication so that they have a voice. Tips: always include choice, and give as much control to the student as possible.

Always think about yourself, your child or a sibling when dealing with a student's appearance. Would you want your child walking around with ketchup on their face?

Always consider discomfort and pain before behavior change. The student may require support to function on a daily basis—your job is to create independence. Autistics individuals often become frustrated with too much prompting. Take a step back and see if they calm down with a little space. Find ways to allow them to function independently.

Fluency Drill for Professional Conduct and Scope of Practice

1.)   RBTs always ___Implement___ program they do not ___Design / Create___ programs.

2.)   ___Behavioral Skills Training___ is a researched method to train parents and staff.

3.)   A ___Multiple Relationship___ is when a therapist enters into a relationship with a student outside of work.

4.)   ___Feedback___ as an opportunity to improve your skills.

5.)   You should always treat a student in the same manner you would treat a ___Family Member___.

Answers to Fluency Drills

Fluency Questions for Measurement Answers

- 1.) Duration
- 2.) Momentary Time Sampling
- 3.) Discontinuous Measurement Procedure or Interval Procedure
- 4.) Latency
- 5.) Whole Interval Recording
- 6.) Frequency, rate
- 7.) Partial Interval Recording
- 8.) Continuous
- 9.) Permanent Product Recording
- 10.) IRT

Fluency Questions for Assessment Answers

- 1.) Operational Definition
- 2.) Antecedent, Consequence
- 3.) Multiple Stimulus Preference Assessment.
- 4.) Indirect assessment
- 5.) Functional Analysis Assessment
- 6.) Forced Choice or Paired Choice Preference Assessment
- 7.) Skills Assessment, Functional Behavior Assessment
- 8.) Direct FBA
- 9.) Free Operant Preference Assessment
- 10.) Multiple Stimulus Preference Assessment without Replacement

Fluency Questions for Skills Acquisition Answers

1.) Positive Reinforcement

2.) Time Delay Prompting

3.) Negative Punishment

4.) Continuous Reinforcement

5.) Intermittent Reinforcement, or FR3

6.) Visual Prompting

7.) Punishment

8.) Positional Prompting

9.) Most to Least Prompting

10.) Physical Prompting

11.) Task Analysis

12.) Discrimination training

13.) S delta

14.) Backwards Chaining

15.) SD

16.) Discrete Trial Training

17.) Naturalistic Training Procedures

18.) Forwards Chaining

19.) Verbal Prompting

20.) Model Prompting

Fluency Questions for Behavior Reduction Answers

1.) Differential reinforcement of a lower rate (DRL)
2.) Behavior Emergency Plan
3.) Escape behavior
4.) Pain attenuation
5.) Non contingent reinforcement
6.) Differential Reinforcement of Incompatible behavior (DRI)
7.) Task modification
8.) Behavior momentum
9.) Sensory behavior
10.) Behavior Reduction Plan, Behavior Intervention Plan.

Fluency Questions for Documenting and Reporting

1.) Incident Report
2.) Team meetings
3.) 24 Hours
4.) Professional language
5.) Ecological Variables

Fluency Questions for Professional Conduct and Scope of Practice

1.) Implement, design or create
2.) Behavioral Skills Training
3.) Multiple Relationship
4.) Feedback
5.) Family Member

Crossword Puzzles

Name: _____   Date: _____

ABA 1

Across

3. A sequence of behaviors that must be performed correctly.

6. Training begins the link with the last behavior in the sequence.

7. Also known as planned ignoring. Ignore the behavior and provide no attention for the behavior.

8. This is a type of data collection in which you record what happened before the behavior occurred (antecedent), record what the behavior looked like (behavior) and record the what happened immediately after the behavior (consequence).

Down

1. The effectiveness of the reinforcer is dependent on the learning history. Things that differ from one person to another, such as music, specific types of food, electronics. Also known as secondary reinforcers.

2. This is when something is made less valuable by satiation.

4. Baselining is finding out where a client's skills or behaviors are before beginning therapy. Before beginning to teach a new skill, a baseline probe should be conducted in order to identify whether the learner already has the skill.

5. Giving the client a choice during therapy, choice increases compliance and provides the learner a sense of control.

Name: _____   Date: _____

ABA 2

Across

3. This is reinforcing a behavior that meets the same function of the maladaptive behavior.

5. These are skills that people use every day to function. They include personal hygiene and grooming, dressing and undressing, meal preparation and eating, moving around the community, toileting, housekeeping, laundry, and safety skills.

6. This is a technique where you increase the demand over time; used to decrease behaviors with the function of escape.

8. Reinforcing another behavior other than the maladaptive behavior.

Down

1. A stimulus in the presence of which a particular response will be reinforced.

2. This procedure involves reinforcing one behavior and extinguishing the behavior (not reinforcing) in the presence of other stimuli.

4. Reinforcing a behavior that cannot physically be engaged in at the same time as the maladaptive behavior.

7. This is typically reserved for behaviors that are socially acceptable but may occur too often.

Name: _____   Date: _____

ABA 3

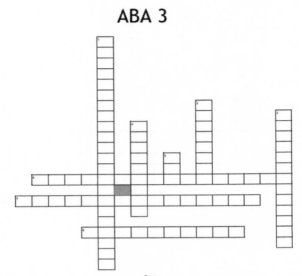

Across

6. Do not allow the client to escape. Physical prompt the client into compliance.
7. Training begins the link with the first behavior in the sequence.
8. Providing reinforcement on a fixed response ratio.

Down

1. This refers to instances when something is made more valuable by deprivation
2. This is how long a behavior occurs. To take duration data you start a stop watch when the behavior begins and end the stop watch when the behavior stops.
3. Providing reinforcement on an interval fixed time ratio.
4. This is a simple count of the instances of behavior, represented by a tally.
5. A teaching method in which learning trials are presented in quick succession, with a clear beginning and clear end to each trial. There are three parts to a discrete trial.

Name: _____   Date: _____

ABA 4

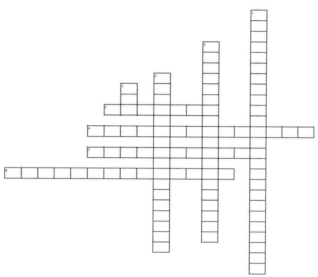

Across

5. the time from prompt to the start of the behavior. To take latency data start the stopwatch when the prompt is given and stop the stopwatch when the behavior starts.

6. Spreading the effects of training to other trainings and settings critical to ensure that ABA effects do not only take place during ABA training.

7. Probing the client to ensure that they still are able to do mastered skills.

8. A prompt where you indicate the correct response by gesturing in some way.

Down

1. All other schedules when reinforcement does not occur after every response.

2. are where you give the learner full physical guidance.

3. This is the time between responses. To take IRT data you start the stop watch when the behavior ends and stop the stop watch when the behavior begins again.

4. A functional behavior assessment is a set of procedures used to determine why someone is engaging in maladaptive behavior.

Name: _____   Date: _____

ABA 5

Across

5. A prompt in which you demonstrate the desired response.
6. A prompt in which you provide some amount of physical assistance in order to help the learner do the expected behavior.
7. removing something from the environment to increase the future probability of the behavior occurring.
8. Taking something away that will increase the future probability that the behavior will decrease

Down

1. This is providing reinforcement to a client regardless of behavior. This will act as an abolishing operation on the reinforcer.
2. Detailed definition of the behavior in observable terms. Must be thorough enough that any person could read it and understand what the behavior is and begin collecting data on the behavior.
3. Introducing something that will increase the future probability that the behavior will decrease.
4. the presence or absence of a behavior during a brief interval of time. intervals are marked as "+" if the target behavior occurred at any time during the interval. intervals are marked as "-" if the target behavior did not occur during the entire interval.

The Behavior Technician Study Guide

ABA 6

Across

4. is a frequency count with a time element.
6. adding something to the environment to increase the future probability of the behavior occurring.
7. A stimulus in the presence of which a particular response will not be reinforced.
8. When one behavior occurs in the presence of a stimulus and then another behavior occurs in the presence of the stimulus.

Down

1. A set of procedures used to determine if one or more stimuli may function to increase the rate of a specific behavior or behaviors when delivered following the occurrence of that behavior.
2. Any consequence that increases a behavior.
3. A prompt where the stimulus that corresponds to the correct response is placed closer to the learner than other stimuli.
5. Any consequence that decreases a behavior.

Name: ....   Date: ....

ABA 7

Across

3. determine where a client's skills are. They typically assess areas such as social skills, coping skills, self-help skills, language skills, learning skills, daily living skills, communications skills.

4. Engaging in behavior to gain something positive in the body.

5. Defined as differentially reinforcing successive approximations toward a terminal behavior

6. Do not provide access to the item during the behavior.

7. This technique is changing how the client does work. Also used for behavior with the function of escape.

8. skills used to communicate and interact with people. Social skills include verbal and non-verbal communication, body language and personal appearance.

Down

1. Occurs when stimuli that share similar physical characteristics with the controlling stimulus evoke the same behavior as the controlling stimulus.

2. Occurs when new stimuli — similar or not similar — to the controlling stimulus do not evoke the same response as the controlling stimulus.

Name: _____   Date: _____

ABA 8

Across

7. Providing reinforcement on a variable (average) time ratio.

8. You can also insert a time delay that occurs after instruction but before the prompt

Down

1. are reinforcement systems that employ a monetary system (token reinforcers) and backup reinforcer.

2. Often used to help clients with transitions and schedules.

3. Providing reinforcement on a variable response ratio.

4. Recording the presence or absence of a behavior during the whole interval. Intervals are marked as "+" if the target behavior occurred during the entire interval. Intervals are marked as "-" if the target behavior stopped at any time during the interval.

5. Supplementary words, instructions, or questions to assist a learner in demonstrating a correct response are called verbal prompts.

6. Training is provided for every behavior in the sequence during every training session.

Answers to Crossword Puzzles

Name: _____   Date: _____

ABA 1

Across

3. A sequence of behaviors that must be performed correctly.
6. Training begins the link with the last behavior in the sequence.
7. Also known as planned ignoring. Ignore the behavior and provide no attention for the behavior.
8. This is a type of data collection in which you record what happened before the behavior occurred (antecedent), record what the behavior looked like (behavior) and record the what happened immediately after the behavior (consequence).

Down

1. The effectiveness of the reinforcer is dependent on the learning history. Things that differ from one person to another, such as music, specific types of food, electronics. Also known as secondary reinforcers.
2. This is when something is made less valuable by satiation.
4. Baselining is finding out where a client's skills or behaviors are before beginning therapy. Before beginning to teach a new skill, a baseline probe should be conducted in order to identify whether the learner already has the skill.
5. Giving the client a choice during therapy, choice increases compliance and provides the learner a sense of control.

Name: ______________________ Date: ____________

ABA 2

Across

3. This is reinforcing a behavior that meets the same function of the maladaptive behavior.

5. These are skills that people use every day to function. They include personal hygiene and grooming, dressing and undressing, meal preparation and eating, moving around the community, toileting, housekeeping, laundry, and safety skills.

6. This is a technique where you increase the demand over time; used to decrease behaviors with the function of escape.

8. Reinforcing another behavior other than the maladaptive behavior.

Down

1. A stimulus in the presence of which a particular response will be reinforced.

2. This procedure involves reinforcing one behavior and extinguishing the behavior (not reinforcing) in the presence of other stimuli.

4. Reinforcing a behavior that cannot physically be engaged in at the same time as the maladaptive behavior.

7. This is typically reserved for behaviors that are socially acceptable but may occur too often.

Name: _____   Date: _____

ABA 3

Across

6. Do not allow the client to escape. Physical prompt the client into compliance.
7. Training begins the link with the first behavior in the sequence.
8. Providing reinforcement on a fixed response ratio.

Down

1. This refers to instances when something is made more valuable by deprivation
2. This is how long a behavior occurs. To take duration data you start a stop watch when the behavior begins and end the stop watch when the behavior stops.
3. Providing reinforcement on an interval fixed time ratio.
4. This is a simple count of the instances of behavior, represented by a tally.
5. A teaching method in which learning trials are presented in quick succession, with a clear beginning and clear end to each trial. There are three parts to a discrete trial.

Name: _____   Date: _____

ABA 4

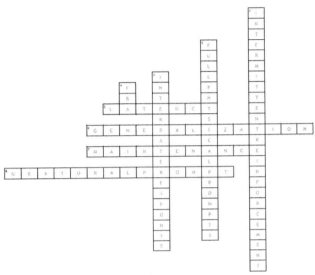

Across

5. the time from prompt to the start of the behavior. To take latency data start the stopwatch when the prompt is given and stop the stopwatch when the behavior starts.

6. Spreading the effects of training to other trainings and settings critical to ensure that ABA effects do not only take place during ABA training.

7. Probing the client to ensure that they still are able to do mastered skills.

8. A prompt where you indicate the correct response by gesturing in some way.

Down

1. All other schedules when reinforcement does not occur after every response.

2. are where you give the learner full physical guidance.

3. This is the time between responses. To take IRT data you start the stop watch when the behavior ends and stop the stop watch when the behavior begins again.

4. A functional behavior assessment is a set of procedures used to determine why someone is engaging in maladaptive behavior.

Name: _____   Date: _____

ABA 5

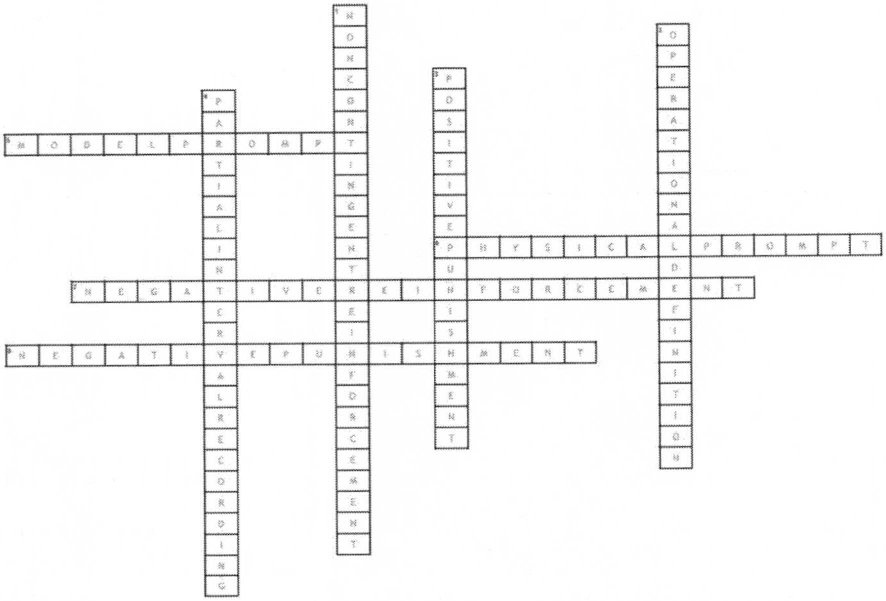

The crossword grid contains the following answers:

Down
1. NONCONTINGENT
2. POSITIVEPUNISHMENT
3. POSITIVEREINFORCEMENT
4. PARTIALINTERVALRECORDING

Across
5. MODELPROMPT
6. PHYSICALPROMPT
7. NEGATIVEREINFORCEMENT
8. NEGATIVEPUNISHMENT

Across
5. A prompt in which you demonstrate the desired response.
6. A prompt in which you provide some amount of physical assistance in order to help the learner do the expected behavior.
7. removing something from the environment to increase the future probability of the behavior occurring.
8. Taking something away that will increase the future probability that the behavior will decrease

Down
1. This is providing reinforcement to a client regardless of behavior. This will act as an abolishing operation on the reinforcer.
2. Detailed definition of the behavior in observable terms. Must be thorough enough that any person could read it and understand what the behavior is and begin collecting data on the behavior.
3. Introducing something that will increase the future probability that the behavior will decrease.
4. the presence or absence of a behavior during a brief interval of time. intervals are marked as "+" if the target behavior occurred at any time during the interval. intervals are marked as "-" if the target behavior did not occur during the entire interval.

The Behavior Technician Study Guide

Name: _____   Date: _____

ABA 6

Across

4. is a frequency count with a time element.

6. adding something to the environment to increase the future probability of the behavior occurring.

7. A stimulus in the presence of which a particular response will not be reinforced.

8. When one behavior occurs in the presence of a stimulus and then another behavior occurs in the presence of the stimulus.

Down

1. A set of procedures used to determine if one or more stimuli may function to increase the rate of a specific behavior or behaviors when delivered following the occurrence of that behavior.

2. Any consequence that increases a behavior.

3. A prompt where the stimulus that corresponds to the correct response is placed closer to the learner than other stimuli.

5. Any consequence that decreases a behavior.

70

Name: _____   Date: _____

ABA 7

Across

3. determine where a client's skills are. They typically assess areas such as social skills, coping skills, self-help skills, language skills, learning skills, daily living skills, communications skills.

4. Engaging in behavior to gain something positive in the body.

5. Defined as differentially reinforcing successive approximations toward a terminal behavior

6. Do not provide access to the item during the behavior.

7. This technique is changing how the client does work. Also used for behavior with the function of escape.

8. skills used to communicate and interact with people. Social skills include verbal and non-verbal communication, body language and personal appearance.

Down

1. Occurs when stimuli that share similar physical characteristics with the controlling stimulus evoke the same behavior as the controlling stimulus.

2. Occurs when new stimuli — similar or not similar — to the controlling stimulus do not evoke the same response as the controlling stimulus.

Name: _____   Date: _____

ABA 8

Across

7. Providing reinforcement on a variable (average) time ratio.

8. You can also insert a time delay that occurs after instruction but before the prompt

Down

1. are reinforcement systems that employ a monetary system (token reinforcers) and backup reinforcer.

2. Often used to help clients with transitions and schedules.

3. Providing reinforcement on a variable response ratio.

4. Recording the presence or absence of a behavior during the whole interval. Intervals are marked as "+" if the target behavior occurred during the entire interval. Intervals are marked as "-" if the target behavior stopped at any time during the interval.

5. Supplementary words, instructions, or questions to assist a learner in demonstrating a correct response are called verbal prompts.

6. Training is provided for every behavior in the sequence during every training session.

Glossary

Abolishing Operation This is when something is made less valuable by satiation.

Access to Something in the Environment A student is engaging in behavior to gain something positive in the environment.

Access to Something in the Body This is sensory behavior. It is engaging in behavior to gain something positive in the body.

Analog or Functional Analysis Assessment This is when a Behavior Analyst manipulates the environment to determine the function of the behavior.

Antecedent Behavior Consequence Data Collection (ABC) This is a type of data collection in which you record what happened before the behavior occurred (antecedent), record what the behavior looked like (behavior) and record the what happened immediately after the behavior (consequence).

Attention Extinction Also known as planned ignoring. Ignore the behavior and provide no attention for the behavior.

Backwards Chaining Training begins the link with the last behavior in the sequence.

Baseline Baselining is finding out where a student's skills or behaviors are before beginning therapy. Before beginning to teach a new skill, a baseline probe should be conducted in order to identify whether the learner already has the skill.

Behavior Chain A sequence of behaviors that must be performed correctly.

Behavioral Skills Training Is a researched based training technique.

Choice Giving the student a choice during therapy, choice increases compliance and provides the learner a sense of control.

Conditioned Reinforcers The effectiveness of the reinforcer is dependent on the learning history. Things that differ from one student to another, such as music, specific types of food, electronics. Also known as secondary reinforcers.

Continuous Measurement Procedures Continuous measurement means measuring each and every instance of behavior within the observation period.

Curriculum-Based Assessment Curriculum-based assessment (CBA) and curriculum-based measurement (CBM) are the repeated, direct assessment of targeted skills in basic areas, such as math, reading, writing, and spelling.

Daily Living Skills These are skills that people use every day to function. They include student hygiene and grooming, dressing and undressing, meal preparation and eating, moving around the community, toileting, housekeeping, laundry, and safety skills.

Demand Fading This is a technique where you increase the demand over time; used to decrease behaviors with the function of escape.

Differential Reinforcement of Alternative Behavior (DRA) This is reinforcing a behavior that meets the same function of the maladaptive behavior.

Differential Reinforcement of Incompatible Behavior (DRI) Reinforcing a behavior that cannot physically be engaged in at the same time as the maladaptive behavior.

Differential Reinforcing Lower Rates of Behavior (DRL) This is typically reserved for behaviors that are socially acceptable but may occur too often.

Differential Reinforcement of Other Behavior (DRO) Reinforcing another behavior other than the maladaptive behavior.

Direct FBA Procedures Part of an FBA will include direct observations and skill assessments. These procedures involve observing the student and recording what is seen.

Discriminative Stimuli (SD) A stimulus in the presence of which a particular response will be reinforced.

Discrimination Training This procedure involves reinforcing one behavior and extinguishing the behavior (not reinforcing) in the presence of other stimuli.

Discontinuous Measurement Procedures Discontinuous Measurement Procedures are samples of the target behavior, but it does not measure every instance of behavior within the observation period.

Discrete Trail Training (DTT) a teaching method in which learning trials are presented in quick succession, with a clear beginning and clear end to each trial. There are three parts to a discrete trial.

Duration This is how long a behavior occurs. To take duration data you start a stop watch when the behavior begins and end the stop watch when the behavior stops.

Escape Extinction Do not allow the student to escape. Physical prompt the student into compliance.

Escaping Something in the Body This is also known as pain attenuation. This refers to engaging in behavior to escape something aversive in the body.

Escaping Something in the Environment A student engages in behavior to escape something aversive in the environment.

Establishing Operations This refers to instances when something is made more valuable by deprivation.

Fixed Interval (FI) Providing reinforcement on a fixed time. Reinforcing the first response correct after a fixed amount of time elapses.

Fixed Ratio (FR) Providing reinforcement on a fixed response ratio.

Forward Chaining Training begins the link with the first behavior in the sequence.

Free Operant Preference Assessment The therapist does not interact with the student. The therapist observes which items the student interacts with and records the time spent with the item.

Frequency This is a simple count of the instances of behavior, represented by a tally.

Full physical prompts are where you give the learner full physical guidance.

Functional Behavior Assessment (FBA) A functional behavior assessment is a set of procedures used to determine why someone is engaging in maladaptive behavior.

Generalization Spreading the effects of training to other trainings and settings critical to ensure that ABA effects do not only take place during ABA training.

Gestural Prompt A prompt where you indicate the correct response by gesturing in some way.

High Probability Sequence/Behavior Momentum Providing 3-4 demands with high compliance (you are sure the learner can and will do them), and presenting the demand with low compliance at the end of the sequence.

Indirect FBA Procedures Part of an FBA may include record reviews, interviews, and rating scales. There is very little contact with the student.

Intermittent Reinforcement All other schedules when reinforcement does not occur after every response.

Inter Rate Response This is the time between responses. To take IRT data you start the stop watch when the behavior ends and stop the stop watch when the behavior begins again.

Latency Latency is the time from prompt to the start of the behavior. To take latency data start the stopwatch when the prompt is given and stop the stopwatch when the behavior starts.

Least-to-Most Prompt Fading Includes procedures where fewer prompts are provided at the beginning of a teaching interaction and gradually more intrusive prompts are faded in when the learner needs help.

Maintenance Probing the student to ensure that they still are able to do mastered skills.

Model prompt A prompt in which you demonstrate the desired response.

Momentary Time Sampling Recording the presence or absence of a behavior at the very end of an interval. Intervals are marked as "+" if the target behavior occurred at the end of the interval. Intervals are marked as "-" when the target behavior does not occur at the end of the interval.

Most to Least Prompt Fading This prompt works in the reverse direction. With MTL prompt fading, you begin the teaching interaction by providing a prompt that you are sure will help the learner make the correct response; then you fade the prompts out.

Multiple Stimulus Preference Assessment with Replacement The therapist presents multiple items at a time and records which item the student chooses to interact with. Once the item is chosen the therapist places it back into the mix of multiple items.

Multiple Stimulus Preference Assessment without Replacement The therapist presents multiple items at a time and records which item the student chooses to interact with. Allow the student to interact with the item for 30 seconds. Once an item is chosen the therapist does not place it back into the array.

Naturalistic Training Procedures Uses natural techniques, and its delivery and can be embedded within play or every day routines.

Negative Punishment Taking something away that will increase the future probability that the behavior will decrease.

Negative Reinforcement Negative reinforcement is removing something from the environment to increase the future probability of the behavior occurring.

Non-Contingent Reinforcement This is providing reinforcement to a student regardless of behavior. This will act as an abolishing operation on the reinforcer.

Operational Definition Detailed definition of the behavior in observable terms. Must be thorough enough that any student could read it and understand what the behavior is and begin collecting data on the behavior.

Paired Choice Preference Assessment (Forced Choice Preference Assessment) The therapist presents 2 items to the student and records which item the student chooses.

Partial physical prompt is a physical prompt in which less than the full amount of physical assistance is provided.

Partial Interval Recording the presence or absence of a behavior during a brief interval of time. Intervals are marked as "+" if the target behavior occurred at any time during the interval. Intervals are marked as "-" if the target behavior did not occur during the entire interval.

Permanent Product Procedures Permanent product recording is not recording behaviors but recording the products behavior produces.

Physical prompt A prompt in which you provide some amount of physical assistance in order to help the learner do the expected behavior.

Positive Punishment Introducing something that will increase the future probability that the behavior will decrease.

Positive Reinforcement Positive reinforcement is adding something to the environment to increase the future probability of the behavior occurring.

Preference Assessment A set of procedures used to determine if one or more stimuli may function to increase the rate of a specific behavior or behaviors when delivered following the occurrence of that behavior.

Proximity Prompt A prompt where the stimulus that corresponds to the correct response is placed closer to the learner than other stimuli.

Punisher Any consequence that decreases a behavior.

Rate Rate is a frequency count with a time element.

Reinforcer Any consequence that increases a behavior.

Response Generalization When one behavior occurs in the presence of a stimulus and then another behavior occurs in the presence of the stimulus.

S-Delta A stimulus in the presence of which a particular response will not be reinforced.

Sensory Engaging in behavior to gain something positive in the body.

Shaping Defined as differentially reinforcing successive approximations toward a terminal behavior.

Single Item Preference Assessment The therapist simply presents one item after another. The therapist records whether the student consumed/interacted with the item, made no response to the item, or avoided the item.

Skill Assessments Skills assessments determine where a student's skills are. They typically assess areas such as social skills, coping skills, self-help skills, language skills, learning skills, daily living skills, communications skills.

Social Skills Social skills are skills used to communicate and interact with people. Social skills include verbal and non-verbal communication, body language and student appearance.

Stimulus Discrimination Occurs when new stimuli — similar or not similar — to the controlling stimulus do not evoke the same response as the controlling stimulus.

Stimulus Generalization Occurs when stimuli that share similar physical characteristics with the controlling stimulus evoke the same behavior as the controlling stimulus.

Tangible Extinction Do not provide access to the item during the behavior.

Task Modification This technique is changing how the student does work. Also used for behavior with the function of escape.

Time Delay Prompt Fading You can also insert a time delay that occurs after instruction but before the prompt.

Token economies are reinforcement systems that employ a monetary system (token reinforcers) and backup reinforcer.

Total Task Chaining Training is provided for every behavior in the sequence during every training session.

Variable Interval (VI) Providing reinforcement on a variable (average) time ratio.

Variable Ratio (VR) Providing reinforcement on a variable response ratio.

Verbal Prompt Supplementary words, instructions, or questions to assist a learner in demonstrating a correct response are called verbal prompts.

Visual Prompt Often used to help students with transitions and schedules.

Whole Interval Recording the presence or absence of a behavior during the whole interval.

Intervals are marked as "+" if the target behavior occurred during the entire interval.

Intervals are marked as "-" if the target behavior stopped at any time during the interval.

Appendix A: Useful Websites

Companion site to this Study Guide
https://www.abastudyguide.com

Free RBT Exam Questions
https://www.abarocks.com

BACB information about the RBT certification
https://www.bacb.com/rbt/

RBT Task list 2.0
https://www.bacb.com/wp-content/uploads/RBT-2nd-Edition-Task-List_181214.pdf

RBT Ethics Code
https://www.bacb.com/wp-content/uploads/RBT-2nd-Edition-Task-List_181214.pdf

RBT competency exam
https://www.bacb.com/wp-content/uploads/RBT_Competency_Assessment_Initial_181226.pdf

RBT training requirements
https://www.bacb.com/rbt-requirements-effective-november-2019/

RBT Exam Information
https://www.bacb.com/rbt/rbt-exam/

References

Baer, D. M., Wolf, M.M., and Risley, T. R. Some current dimensions of applied behavior analysis. *Journal of Applied Behavior Analysis*, 1, 91–97, 1968.

Behavior Analyst Certification Board. (2018). Registered Behavior Technician™ (RBT™) Task List, 2018. *<https://www.bacb.com/wp-content/uploads/RBT-2nd-Edition-Task-List_181214.pdf>*

Behavior Analyst Certification Board. Registered Behavior Technician Ethics Code™ (RBT™), 2018. *<https://www.bacb.com/wp-content/uploads/RBT-Ethics-Code_190227.pdf>*

Cooper, J. H., Heward, W. L., and Heron, T. E. *Applied Behavior Analysis*. Upper Saddle River, NJ: Prentice Hall, 2007.

Hanley G. P., Iwata B. A., and McCord B. E. Functional analysis of problem, Wiley, 2003.

Malott, D. W., and Joseph, S. T. *Principles of Behavior*. Boston: Pearson, 2014.

Made in the USA
Columbia, SC
04 March 2021